the salt plate cookbook

WILLIAMS-SONOMA
test kitchen

photographs Maren Caruso

weldon**owen**

CONTENTS

Welcome to Salt Plate Cooking

The salt plate is a versatile kitchen tool that will change the way you cook, prepare, and serve food. Sourced from Himalayan salt deposits, the dense slab, made from pink salt crystals, adds nutrients and delicate flavor to food. The salt plate can be used in many different ways. For example, you can heat it on the stove top or grill to cook thinly cut meat, poultry, fish, and vegetables; you can warm it in the oven to add a hint of salt flavor to biscuits, cookies, and other items while they bake; you can chill it in the refrigerator or freezer to use for mixing or curing raw foods, or incorporating toppings and an appealing salty note into ice cream; or you can simply use the salt plate as a serving platter for your favorite dishes—it can go from the stove top, oven, grill, refrigerator, or freezer right to the tabletop.

On the pages that follow, you'll find a complete primer on salt plate cooking as well as tips and tricks for making the most of its features. Following are more than 20 recipes, from seared meats to baked treats. Beef Teppanyaki (page 46) is an easy, yet elegant dish that can be prepared right at the table. Or, try a foolproof technique for salt-curing salmon (page 32) for delicious gravlax in just minutes instead of days. You'll also discover new ways to prepare and enjoy your favorite foods, like Cheeseburgers (page 42), Chocolate Chip Cookies (page 49), and more, seasoning each item perfectly while it cooks or bakes. You'll find all of these creative dishes, including appetizers, mains, sides, baked goods, and desserts inside this book to make the most of this innovative tool.

About the Salt Plate

The salt plate is harvested from enormous deposits of Himalayan pink salt that date back millions of years. The salt is rich in minerals and high in natural moisture, which lend lots of flavor to food and allow the salt plate to be heated or chilled to very high and very low temperatures. Each of the salt plate's three main uses create a unique cooking and dining experience.

Hot Food

You can grill, bake, sear, and sauté a wide variety of foods directly on the salt plate. On the grill, the salt plate acts as a flat griddle, allowing you to cook small items that might otherwise fall through the grill grate. In the oven, the salt plate acts as a baking sheet or pizza stone, resulting in crisp, evenly browned, and lightly seasoned baked goods and pizza. On the stove top, the salt plate behaves like a hot frying pan, helping you to sear meat, poultry, fish, and vegetables to a golden brown finish, or sauté items with a light coating of oil.

Cold Food

A chilled or frozen salt plate is an excellent way to serve cold dishes. It keeps food cool and lends a welcome hint of saltiness to dishes prepared on it, like the beef tartare on page 21 or the chocolate bark on page 53. You can also chill or freeze the salt plate to quickly cure fish or mix toppings and add a touch of salty flavor into frozen desserts.

Prepared Food

The salt plate's beautiful pink crystal composition makes it an elegant serving platter, while imparting a subtle saltiness to food served on it. Use a cold salt plate for serving fruit, cheese, sushi, deviled eggs, and more. Or, use a warm salt plate set on a heavy trivet on the table to keep foods warm for serving family style.

What can be prepared on a Salt Plate?

- meat
- poultry
- fish
- shellfish
- vegetables
- fruit
- pizza
- quesadillas
- baked goods
- eggs
- chocolate confections
- frozen treats

Salt Plate Cooking Primer

The salt plate can be heated up to to 500°F for searing, sautéing, grilling, and baking. Whether heating the salt plate on a grill or stove top, or in the oven, the secret to success is heating the plate slowly, which prevents the plate from cracking and ensures even cooking of the food. Heating the salt plate to the proper temperature also prevents too much salt from seeping into the food. After cooking, let the salt plate cool completely on a heatproof surface for 3–8 hours.

Stove Top Cooking: Place the salt plate directly on an unheated gas burner. Turn on the burner to low heat. After 15 minutes, increase the heat to medium. After another 15 minutes, increase the heat to medium-high and allow the salt plate to heat for 15 more minutes before cooking. (The salt plate is not recommended for use on an electric stove.)

Oven Cooking: In a cold oven, move an oven rack to the lower third of the oven and place the salt plate on the rack (do not put the salt plate in a hot oven). Preheat the oven to the temperature called for in the recipe. Allow the plate to warm for 1 hour and 15 minutes before cooking.

Gas Grilling: Place the salt plate on the cooking grate of an unheated grill. Turn on the burner directly below the plate to low heat. Cover the grill and heat until the temperature of the grill reaches 250°F, about 15 minutes. Increase the heat to medium and heat until the grill temperature reaches 400°F, about 15 more minutes, before cooking.

Charcoal Grilling: Prepare a three-zone fire in the grill (low heat on one side, no coals in the middle, medium heat on the other side). Once the coals are ready, place the salt plate on the low heat side and heat for 15 minutes. Move the plate to the medium-heat side and heat for 15 more minutes before cooking.

===== SAFETY TIPS =====

Always use thick oven mitts when handling a hot salt plate. If you are using the salt plate as a serving vessel while it's still hot, use a thick trivet to protect the table or counter top from the heat.

Tips & Tricks

Follow these basic tips for using and caring for your salt plate. Before you start, be sure to consult the manufacturer's instructions for more information.

Chill it: Place the salt plate in the refrigerator for 2 hours. When fully chilled, carefully transfer the plate to a cool surface and use for serving chilled foods. Serve food with high moisture concentrations in a fanned or stacked manner so that only a small edge of the food is in direct contact with the salt plate.

Freeze it: Place the salt plate in the freezer for 2 hours. When fully frozen, carefully transfer it to a cool surface and use for serving chilled and frozen foods.

Heat it: Follow the directions on page 11 to heat the salt plate slowly and evenly.

Prep it: Foods with a high water concentration, such as fruit, seafood, and juicy vegetables, will absorb more salt than foods naturally low in water. Prevent excess saltiness by patting foods dry with a paper towel prior to cooking.

Oil it: To prevent delicate foods, such such as eggs, from sticking to the salt plate when cooking, first drizzle the preheated plate with a thin layer of oil. The oil will provide a barrier between the plate and the food, preventing foods from picking up too much salt.

Keep it small: Small and thinly sliced foods cook best on the salt plate. When cooking meat, opt for thin slices over large roasts. (One exception: a spatchcocked chicken works really well on a salt plate; see page 39.)

Clean it: Using a thin metal spatula, scrape off any food debris from the surface of the salt plate. If the salt plate has been heated, let it cool completely on a heatproof surface for 3–8 hours. Use lukewarm water and a moist sponge or scouring pad to clean the cooled salt plate. Because of the plate's natural anti-microbial qualities, it only needs a minimal scrubbing. Do not soak the salt plate, use soap, or put it in the dishwasher.

Dry it: After cleaning, dry the salt plate thoroughly with paper towels or a clean dish towel. Set the plate on a drying rack or wire rack set on top of a baking sheet to dry completely. The plate should be completely dry before using again.

Preserve it: Because the salt plate is made from 100% natural salt, it will disintegrate over time. After repetitive use, the plate will begin to show some signs of wear in the form of fissures, pigment changes, or, in some cases, the loss of small chunks from the plate. If a portion of the salt plate breaks off, save it and use it to grate over dishes as a finishing salt.

Salt-Grilled Pizza Margarita

The salt plate serves as a flavorful pizza stone on the grill, creating the perfect pizza or flatbread crust. We like a classic margarita pizza (tomato, cheese, and fresh basil), but feel free to use your own favorite toppings.

1 Place the salt plate on the cooking grate of a gas grill and turn on the grill to low heat. (If using a charcoal grill, see page 11 for instructions.) Cover the grill and warm until the internal temperature of the grill reaches 250°F, about 15 minutes. Increase the heat to medium and warm until the internal temperature of the grill reaches 500°F, 20–25 minutes longer.

2 Divide the pizza dough in half. On a well-floured work surface, roll out 1 piece of the dough into an 8-inch round. Transfer the dough round to a lightly floured pizza peel or flat cookie sheet. Spread half of the marinara sauce over the surface of the dough round, leaving a 1-inch border. Top with half of the cheese.

3 Carefully slide the pizza dough from the peel onto the hot salt plate. Close the grill and cook until the pizza is cooked through and the cheese is melted, 8–10 minutes. Carefully slide the pizza back onto the peel and transfer to a cutting board. Sprinkle the pizza with basil and pepper flakes, if using, and serve right away.

4 Repeat to top, cook, garnish, and serve the remaining pizza dough round.

SERVES 4

1 lb prepared pizza dough

All-purpose flour, for rolling

½ cup prepared marinara sauce

4 oz fresh mozzarella cheese, cut into slices

Fresh basil leaves, cut into slivers or torn

Red pepper flakes (optional)

Herb-Marinated Vegetable Skewers

Vegetables pick up a lot of flavor from the salt plate. Here, we've added a bold herb-and-garlic marinade, for vegetable skewers that are bursting with flavor, color, and texture.

2 cloves garlic, minced

2 tablespoons chopped fresh flat-leaf parsley

2 teaspoons finely grated lemon zest

¼ cup fresh lemon juice

¼ cup olive oil

3 tablespoons finely chopped shallot

2 cups grape or cherry tomatoes

2 cups zucchini pieces (1-inch pieces)

1 cup yellow squash pieces (1-inch pieces)

1 red onion, cut into 1-inch chunks

1 red or yellow bell pepper, seeded and cut into 1-inch chunks

½ lb button mushrooms, quartered

1 In a bowl, mix together the garlic, parsley, lemon zest, lemon juice, oil, and shallot to make a marinade. Add the tomatoes, zucchini, yellow squash, onion, bell pepper, and mushrooms to the marinade and let soak for 1 hour.

2 Have ready 8–10 metal skewers, or soak wooden skewers in water for 30 minutes. Place the salt plate on the cooking grate of a gas grill and turn on the grill to low heat. (If using a charcoal grill, see page 11 for instructions.) Cover the grill and warm until the internal temperature of the grill reaches 250°F, about 15 minutes. Increase the heat to medium and warm until the internal temperature of the grill is 400°F, 15–20 minutes longer.

3 Thread the marinated vegetable pieces onto the skewers, alternating types and colors. Place the vegetables directly on the hot salt plate, cover the grill, and cook, turning occasionally, until the vegetables are tender and lightly charred, about 10 minutes. Transfer to a platter and serve right away.

SERVES 4

> ═══ **TIP** ═══
> If your grill does not have a built-in thermometer, look for a grill thermometer at a kitchenware store or online. Follow the manufacturer's instructions for use.

Smashed Potatoes with Chimichurri

The crisp, golden brown exteriors and creamy interiors of these potatoes provide a complimentary foil to the fresh, zingy chimichurri. Pair this side dish with steak, chicken, or fish, or use as part of a vegetarian meal.

1 Set the salt plate on top of a gas burner on the stove top and turn on the heat to low. Warm the plate for 15 minutes. Increase the heat to medium and warm for 15 minutes. Increase the heat to medium-high and warm for 15 more minutes, for a total of 45 minutes.

2 Place the parsley, cilantro, shallots, garlic, salt, and pepper flakes in a food processor and pulse until coarsely chopped, about 10 pulses. Scrape down the sides of the bowl. Add the ½ cup olive oil and the vinegar and pulse until the mixture is the consistency of chunky pesto, 10–12 pulses. Transfer to a bowl.

3 Simmer the potatoes in salted water to cover until just tender when pierced with the tip of a paring knife, about 12 minutes. Drain the potatoes, then transfer to a bowl and toss with the remaining 1 tablespoon oil. Pour the potatoes onto a rimmed baking sheet. Use the bottom of a measuring cup to smash the potatoes evenly until ½-inch thick.

4 Carefully place the potatoes on the hot salt plate and cook until browned and crisp on the bottom, 2–3 minutes. Using a thin metal spatula, turn the potatoes over and cook until browned on the other side, 2–3 minutes longer. Transfer to a bowl and drizzle some chimichurri on top. Reserve the remaining chimichurri for another use.

SERVES 4

¾ cup packed fresh flat-leaf parsley leaves

¼ cup packed fresh cilantro leaves

¼ cup coarsely chopped shallots

2 garlic cloves, minced

1½ teaspoons kosher salt, plus more as needed

¼ teaspoon red pepper flakes

½ cup plus 1 tablespoon extra-virgin olive oil

¼ cup red wine vinegar

1 lb small multicolored or Yukon gold potatoes, about 1 inch in diameter

Chicken, Chile & Corn Quesadillas

These quesadillas come together quickly and are a crowd favorite. Brushing the outside of the tortillas with melted butter ensures a crispy exterior with just a hint of salt. For a complete meal, serve with sliced avocados and pico de gallo or alongside a simple green salad.

¼ lb Cheddar cheese, shredded

¼ lb Monterey jack cheese, shredded

4 burrito-size flour tortillas

Melted butter, for brushing

1 cup cooked, shredded chicken (about 4 oz)

1 cup fresh or thawed frozen corn kernels

1 can (4 oz) diced green chiles, drained

½ cup thinly sliced green onions

1 Place the salt plate on the cooking grate of a gas grill and turn on the grill to low heat. (If using a charcoal grill, see page 11 for instructions.) Cover the grill and warm until the internal temperature of the grill reaches 250°F, about 15 minutes. Increase the heat to medium and warm until the internal temperature of the grill reaches 400°F, 15–20 minutes longer.

2 In a small bowl, toss together the Cheddar and Monterey jack cheeses. Place the tortillas flat on a work surface and brush 1 side of each tortilla with melted butter. Turn the tortillas buttered-side down on the work surface. Using half of the cheese mixture, divide it among the tortillas, covering one-half of each tortilla. Top the cheese with the chicken, corn, chiles, and green onions, dividing each equally among the tortillas. Top with the remaining cheese mixture, dividing evenly. Fold the uncovered half of each tortilla over the filling and press to enclose the filling.

3 Working in batches, carefully transfer the quesadillas to the hot salt plate. Cook, turning once, until the cheese is melted and the tortilla is browned and crisp, about 3 minutes per side.

4 Transfer each quesadilla to a cutting board, cut into wedges, and serve right away.

SERVES 4

Beef Tartare

This recipe uses a salt plate for seasoning and then serving beef tartare. The water released from the beef naturally pulls the salt out of the plate. Adjust the time the tartare sits on the salt plate according to your taste, keeping in mind that the longer the food sits, the saltier it will become.

1 Place the salt plate in the refrigerator and chill until very cold, about 2 hours.

2 Trim the steak well and then finely chop it. Place the chopped steak in a bowl. Drizzle the steak with the olive oil and mix well. Add the shallot, parsley, capers, Worcestershire sauce, and 2–3 dashes hot sauce, or to taste. Holding the egg yolk in your hand over the bowl, gently squeeze the yolk until it bursts, then drizzle it over the beef mixture. Discard any albumen (egg white) left in your hand. Stir the mixture well. Season the mixture with pepper to taste and mix well.

3 Transfer the beef mixture to the chilled salt plate, spreading it out into a ½- to ¾-inch layer. Transfer the salt plate to the refrigerator for 30 minutes to 1 hour.

4 Remove the salt plate from the refrigerator and serve right away with crostini.

SERVES 4–6

12 oz best-quality New York strip steak

1 tablespoon extra-virgin olive oil

1½ tablespoons finely chopped shallot

1½ tablespoons finely chopped fresh flat-leaf parsley

¼ cup capers, drained and roughly chopped

1 teaspoon Worcestershire sauce

Hot-pepper sauce, such as Tabasco

1 egg yolk

Freshly ground pepper

Crostini, for serving

TIP

This recipe uses uncooked steak and egg yolk, so be sure they are impeccably fresh. Do not consume raw foods if you have food safety concerns.

Quinoa, Tomato & Feta-Stuffed Portobellos

A great use for leftover quinoa, these stuffed portobellos make for a healthful and filling vegetarian main dish. For a twist, try substituting goat cheese for feta or another cooked vegetable for the kale.

1 cup cooked quinoa (see Tip)

¼ bunch lacinato kale (about 2 oz), stemmed, and very thinly sliced (about ⅔ cup)

½ pint cherry tomatoes, halved lengthwise

2 oz feta cheese, crumbled

2 tablespoons olive oil, plus more for drizzling

1 tablespoon fresh lemon juice

Kosher salt and freshly ground pepper

4 portobello mushrooms, each 3–4 inches in diameter, stems and gills removed

1 Place the salt plate on an oven rack set on the bottom third of the oven. Turn on the oven to 400°F and set a timer for 1 hour 15 minutes.

2 In a large bowl, toss together the quinoa, kale, tomatoes, feta cheese, 2 tablespoons oil, and the lemon juice. Season to taste with salt and pepper.

3 Lightly drizzle both sides of the portobellos with olive oil. Place the portobellos cap-side down and divide the quinoa mixture among them, using your hand to gently pack the stuffing into the cavities. Carefully transfer the stuffed mushrooms to the hot salt plate. Bake until the mushrooms are tender and the stuffing is lightly browned, 20–25 minutes. Serve warm or at room temperature.

SERVES 4

> === TIP ===
>
> To cook quinoa, in a small saucepan over medium-high heat, warm 1 tablespoon olive oil. Add 1 cup uncooked rinsed quinoa and cook, stirring occasionally, until lightly toasted, 2–3 minutes. Add 1¾ cups water or broth and a pinch of salt. Bring to a boil, then reduce heat to low, cover, and cook until all the water has been absorbed, about 20 minutes. Fluff with a fork. You'll only use 1 cup for this recipe; reserve the rest for another use.

Salt & Black Pepper Drop Biscuits

Lightly brushing the hot salt plate with melted butter before dropping
the dough on top ensures that the biscuits develop irresistibly well
browned and crisp bottoms that release easily from the salt plate.

1 Place the salt plate on an oven rack set in the bottom
third of the oven. Turn on the oven to 400°F and set
a timer for 1 hour 15 minutes.

2 After 1 hour has elapsed, prepare the biscuit dough:
In a bowl, combine the flour, baking powder, sugar,
salt, and pepper and whisk together. Using a pastry
blender or two knives, cut the butter pieces into the
flour mixture until they are the size of peas. Pour in
the buttermilk and stir just until combined.

3 Using oven mitts, carefully remove the salt plate from
the oven and set on the counter on top of a wire rack.
Brush the top of the salt plate with some of the melted
butter. Using a ⅓-cup measure, drop the biscuit dough
onto the plate in 3 rows of 3, spacing them evenly
apart. Return the salt plate to the oven and bake until
a toothpick inserted into the center of a biscuit comes
out clean, 18–20 minutes.

4 Remove the salt plate from the oven and set it on
the wire rack. Brush the tops of the biscuits with the
remaining melted butter. Using a metal spatula, transfer
the biscuits onto another wire rack. Let cool for 10 minutes
before serving.

MAKES 9 BISCUITS

2 cups all-purpose flour

1 tablespoon baking powder

2 teaspoons sugar

¾ teaspoon table salt

½ teaspoon freshly ground black pepper

½ cup (1 stick) cold unsalted butter, cut into ½-inch pieces, plus 2 tablespoons butter, melted

1 cup buttermilk

Salt-Seared Sea Scallops

A hot salt plate lends a perfect sear to delicate sea scallops while seasoning them nicely. For a light lunch or dinner, serve the scallops with a citrus and arugula salad tossed with lemon vinaigrette.

1 lb large sea scallops

Freshly ground black pepper

½ lemon

1 Set the salt plate on top of a gas burner on the stove top and turn on the heat to low. Warm the plate for 15 minutes. Increase the heat to medium and warm for 15 minutes. Increase the heat to medium-high and warm for 15 more minutes, for a total of 45 minutes.

2 Sprinkle the scallops on both sides with pepper. Place the scallops on the hot salt plate and cook for 2 minutes. Flip the scallops, squeeze the juice from the lemon half over the top, and continue to cook until the scallops are just firm to the touch and still slightly translucent in the center, about 2 minutes longer. Serve right away.

SERVES 4

=== **TIP** ===

Do not pat the scallops dry before cooking them. The moisture on the scallops allows for more salt to come through when cooking on the salt plate.

Coconut-Curry Shrimp Skewers

These flavor-packed shrimp skewers are crowd-pleasers, not to mention fast and easy. Serve with steamed basmati rice and green beans sautéed with a little fresh ginger and chopped chiles.

1 Have ready 16–20 metal skewers, or soak wooden skewers in water for 30 minutes.

2 Place the salt plate on the cooking grate of a gas grill and turn on the grill to low heat. (If using a charcoal grill, see page 11 for instructions.) Cover the grill and warm until the internal temperature of the grill reaches 250°F, about 15 minutes. Increase the heat to medium and warm until the internal temperature of the grill reaches 500°F, 25–30 minutes longer.

3 Near the end of the heating process, quickly marinate the shrimp: In a bowl, combine the coconut milk, curry powder, garlic powder, onion powder, ground ginger, cayenne, lime zest, and lime juice. Add the shrimp, toss well, and marinate for 8–10 minutes.

4 Thread the shrimp onto the skewers, threading 1 skewer near the head and 1 skewer near the tail of each shrimp. Place the shrimp skewers on the hot salt plate and cook until the shrimp are pink and firm, flipping them halfway through, 1–2 minutes per side. Serve right away with limes for squeezing.

SERVES 4

½ cup coconut milk

4 teaspoons curry powder

½ teaspoon garlic powder

½ teaspoon onion powder

½ teaspoon ground ginger

¼ teaspoon cayenne pepper

Finely grated zest of 1 lime

1 tablespoon fresh lime juice

1 lb medium shrimp, peeled and deveined, tails intact

Lime quarters, for serving

=== **TIP** ===
Threading the shrimp onto 2 skewers keeps them from twirling on the skewers as you turn them.

Salt-and-Pepper Peel 'n' Eat Shrimp

The salt plate brings out the subtle salinity found in many types of seafood. For a great accompaniment to this dish, butter ears of fresh corn and sear them on the hot salt plate until browned, turning to cook all sides.

1 lb medium shrimp, deveined, shells and tails intact

1 teaspoon coarsely ground black pepper

1 Place the salt plate on the cooking grate of a gas grill and turn on the grill to low heat. (If using a charcoal grill, see page 11 for instructions.) Cover the grill and warm until the internal temperature of the grill reaches 250°F, about 15 minutes. Increase the heat to medium and warm until the internal temperature of the grill reaches 500°F, 25–30 minutes longer.

2 Rinse the shrimp with cool water and drain well. Sprinkle the shrimp evenly with the pepper. Place the shrimp on the hot salt plate and cook until the shrimp are pink and firm, flipping them halfway through, 3–4 minutes.

3 Serve right away, instructing diners to peel the shrimp and eat it with their fingers. Provide a bowl to discard the shells, as well as lots of napkins.

SERVES 4

TIP

To make this recipe fast and easy, ask your fishmonger for shrimp that still has the shell on but has been deveined.

Salmon with Chipotle-Orange Rub

For even cooking, choose salmon fillets that are similar in thickness and squared off in shape, rather than long and skinny. Round out the meal with a black bean, zucchini, and fresh corn salad.

1 Place the salt plate on the cooking grate of a gas grill and turn on the grill to low heat. (If using a charcoal grill, see page 11 for instructions.) Cover the grill and warm until the internal temperature of the grill reaches 250°F, about 15 minutes. Increase the heat to medium and warm until the internal temperature of the grill reaches 400°F, 15–20 minutes longer.

2 In a small bowl, stir together the orange zest, oregano, chipotle powder, onion powder, cumin, coriander, brown sugar, and salt. Stir in the orange juice until a paste forms. Gently rub the paste in an even layer on the flesh side of each fish fillet.

3 Place the fillets flesh-side down on the hot salt plate, cover the grill, and cook until the bottom is well seared, 2 minutes. Turn the fillets flesh-side up and cook about 2 minutes longer for medium rare. Serve right away.

SERVES 4

Finely grated zest of 1 orange (about 1½ teaspoons)

1 teaspoon dried oregano

1 teaspoon chipotle powder

1 teaspoon onion powder

¾ teaspoon ground cumin

½ teaspoon ground coriander

½ teaspoon brown sugar

¼ teaspoon kosher salt

2 teaspoons fresh orange juice

4 skin-on salmon fillets, about 6 oz each

Quick-Cured Salmon with Dill

A Himalayan salt plate is excellent for quick-curing meats and fish. For this recipe, use the freshest, top-quality salmon you can find and ask the fishmonger to slice it for you. Serve it as an appetizer with crostini and herbed crème fraîche, or as a first course with a green salad alongside. Or, serve it with bagels, cream cheese, capers, and thinly sliced red onion.

12 oz fresh salmon, cut into slices ³⁄₁₆ to ¼ inch thick

Sugar, as needed

¼ cup small fresh dill fronds

Freshly ground black pepper

1 Place the salt plate in the refrigerator and chill until very cold, about 2 hours.

2 Place 6 of the salmon slices on a parchment-lined baking sheet. Using about ½ teaspoon of sugar, lightly sprinkle it over the salmon slices. Top each slice with a few dill fronds, then season lightly with pepper. Turn the slices over and repeat using ½ teaspoon more sugar, a few more dill fronds, and pepper.

3 Transfer the seasoned salmon slices in a single layer to the chilled salt plate and let stand for 2 minutes. Turn the slices over and let stand on the salt plate for 2 minutes more. Transfer the salmon to a chilled platter. Working in batches of 6 slices, repeat the process with the remaining salmon slices. Serve right away.

SERVES 2–4

=== **TIP** ===

Be sure to chill the salt plate before using to keep the fish cold and easy to work with. The longer the salmon sits on the plate, the saltier it will become, so adjust the time as desired.

Seared Tuna with Ginger-Soy Dipping Sauce

Cooking fresh tuna on a hot salt plate renders the exterior well seared and nicely seasoned, while the interior remains perfectly pink and rare. Serve with steamed snow peas or another favorite vegetable.

1 Set the salt plate on top of a gas burner on the stove top and turn on the heat to low. Warm the plate for 15 minutes. Increase the heat to medium and warm for 15 minutes. Increase the heat to medium-high and warm for 15 more minutes, for a total of 45 minutes.

2 During the last phase of heating, in a re-sealable plastic bag, combine the mirin, rice vinegar, ginger, and wasabi paste. Add the tuna to the bag, force out the air, and seal. Let the tuna marinate in the refrigerator for 15 minutes.

3 Meanwhile, make the dipping sauce: In a bowl, combine the soy sauce, sesame oil, mirin, rice vinegar, green onion, sesame seeds, and ginger.

4 Place the tuna on the hot salt plate and cook, turning once, until seared on the outside and still rare in the center, about 2½ minutes per side.

5 Cut the tuna across the grain into slices about ½ inch thick. Serve with the dipping sauce.

SERVES 2–4

¼ cup mirin

¼ cup rice vinegar

1 teaspoon freshly grated ginger

1 teaspoon wasabi paste

1 ahi tuna steak, about 1 lb and 1½ inches thick

FOR THE DIPPING SAUCE

½ cup soy sauce

¼ cup toasted sesame oil

4 teaspoons mirin

2 teaspoons rice vinegar

4 teaspoons thinly sliced green onion

2 teaspoons black sesame seeds

1 teaspoon freshly grated ginger

Chicken Satay

Thinly sliced chicken threaded on skewers and served with a tangy peanut sauce is always a crowd-pleaser. To make this recipe a complete meal, serve with a simple cucumber salad and steamed jasmine rice.

½ cup creamy peanut butter

1 teaspoon freshly grated ginger

1 teaspoon minced garlic

Finely grated zest of 1 lime

1 teaspoon fresh lime juice

1 teaspoon Asian fish sauce

1 tablespoon brown sugar

1 lb boneless, skinless chicken thighs, cut into ½-inch strips

Lime wedges, for serving

1 Place the salt plate on the cooking grate of a gas grill and turn on the grill to low heat. (If using a charcoal grill, see page 11 for instructions.) Cover the grill and warm until the internal temperature of the grill reaches 250°F, about 15 minutes. Increase the heat to medium and warm until the internal temperature of the grill reaches 400°F, 15–20 minutes longer.

2 While the salt plate is heating, in a bowl, whisk together the peanut butter, ginger, garlic, lime zest, lime juice, fish sauce, brown sugar, and ¼ cup water until smooth; the mixture will be thick. Thread the chicken evenly onto 8 short or 4 long skewers, place in a large re-sealable plastic bag, and add the peanut mixture. Seal the bag, pressing out any air, and massage the chicken with the peanut mixture until coated. Refrigerate for 30 minutes.

3 Place the skewers on the hot salt plate, cover the grill, and cook until the chicken is lightly charred on the bottom, about 5 minutes. Turn the skewers over and cook until the chicken is lightly charred on the other side and cooked through, about 5 minutes longer. Serve right away with lime wedges for squeezing.

SERVES 4

Lemon-Herb Spatchcocked Chicken

"Spatchcocking" a chicken (removing its backbone and flattening the bird) reduces the cooking time considerably. Here, we cook the flattened chicken on a hot salt plate while weighting it with a heavy frying pan. The result? A perfectly seasoned, whole roasted chicken in just 20 minutes.

1 In a large, re-sealable plastic bag, combine the oil, garlic, shallots, rosemary, thyme, pepper flakes, and lemon zest and juice. Place the chicken in the bag, seal tightly, and refrigerate for 2–24 hours.

2 Remove the chicken from the refrigerator. Place the salt plate on the cooking grate of a gas grill and turn on the grill to low heat. (If using a charcoal grill, see page 11 for instructions.) Cover the grill and warm until the internal temperature of the grill reaches 250°F, about 15 minutes. Increase the heat to medium and warm until the internal temperature of the grill reaches 400°F, 15–20 minutes longer. During last 10 minutes, place a large cast-iron skillet on the grill over medium heat.

3 Remove the chicken from the marinade; discard the marinade. Place the bird, breast-side down, on the hot salt plate. Carefully place the hot frying pan on top and close the grill. Cook until an instant-read thermometer inserted into the thickest part of the thigh, away from the bone, registers 170°F, about 20 minutes. Carefully remove the pan from the bird. Using a spatula, transfer the chicken to a carving board. Tent the bird loosely with foil and let rest for 15 minutes.

4 Place the lemon halves cut-side down on the salt plate and cook until lightly browned, about 2 minutes. Carve the chicken and serve with the seared lemons for squeezing.

SERVES 4

2 tablespoons olive oil

3 cloves garlic, minced

2 shallots, thinly sliced

1 teaspoon chopped fresh rosemary

1 teaspoon chopped fresh thyme

½ teaspoon red pepper flakes

Finely grated zest and juice of 1 lemon, plus 2 whole lemons, halved

1 whole chicken, about 4 lb, backbone removed, wings tucked under, and the bird flattened with your hands

Salt-Fried Eggs with Maple-Sage Breakfast Sausage

Take breakfast outdoors with these quick sausage patties and fried eggs made using the salt plate as a griddle on an outdoor grill. Maple syrup adds a subtle sweetness to the sausage patties. Serve with lightly grilled slices of your favorite bread or English muffins.

1 lb ground pork

¾ teaspoon rubbed sage

½ teaspoon dried thyme

½ teaspoon dried marjoram or oregano

¼ teaspoon ground ginger

Kosher salt and freshly ground pepper

⅛ teaspoon cayenne pepper

1 tablespoon maple syrup

Olive oil, as needed

4 large eggs

1 Place the salt plate on the cooking grate of a gas grill and turn on the grill to low heat. (If using a charcoal grill, see page 11 for instructions.) Cover the grill and warm until the internal temperature of the grill reaches 250°F, about 15 minutes. Increase the heat to medium and warm until the internal temperature of the grill reaches 400°F, 15–20 minutes longer.

2 In a bowl, combine the pork, sage, thyme, marjoram, ginger, ½ teaspoon salt, ¼ teaspoon black pepper, the cayenne pepper, and maple syrup and mix well. Divide the pork mixture into eight equal balls and press each ball into a patty about ¼ inch thick.

3 Working in 2 batches, place the sausage patties on the hot salt plate. Cook, turning once, until lightly browned and cooked through, about 2 minutes per side. Transfer the patties to a plate and loosely tent with foil.

4 Generously drizzle the salt plate with olive oil. Working in 2 batches, crack 2 eggs onto the salt plate and cook until the whites are just set and yolks are still runny, 3–4 minutes, or until done to your liking. Season the eggs with salt and pepper and serve right away with the patties. Repeat with the remaining eggs.

SERVES 4

Pork Tenderloin with Apricot-Mustard Glaze

The salt plate gives the tenderloin a crispy sear while keeping it juicy and tender on the inside. A simple glaze of apricot preserves and grainy mustard brushed onto the pork after cooking lends a pleasing sweet-savory flavor. Serve with cole slaw dressed with apple cider vinaigrette.

1 Place the salt plate on the cooking grate of a gas grill and turn on the grill to low heat. (If using a charcoal grill, see page 11 for instructions.) Cover the grill and warm until the internal temperature of the grill reaches 250°F, about 15 minutes. Increase the heat to medium and warm until the internal temperature of the grill reaches 400°F, 15–20 minutes longer.

2 While the salt plate is heating, make the glaze: In a small saucepan, combine the preserves, mustard, and vinegar and bring to a low boil over medium heat. Stir until smooth. Remove from the heat.

3 Place the tenderloin on the hot salt plate, close the grill, and cook, turning the meat every 5 minutes, until a meat thermometer registers 140°F in the thickest part of the meat, 15–20 minutes. Transfer the tenderloin to a plate and brush the glaze over the surface of the meat. Tent the meat with foil and let rest for 10 minutes.

4 Cut the tenderloin crosswise into 1-inch slices and serve with the remaining glaze drizzled over the top.

SERVES 4–6

¼ cup apricot preserves

2 tablespoons whole-grain mustard

2 tablespoons cider vinegar

1 pork tenderloin, about 1 lb

Salt-Seared Cheeseburgers

Cooking the patties directly on the salt plate not only adds a nice sear to the meat, but also alleviates the need to mix the seasonings into the ground meat mixture before cooking. If you like a bold touch with the salt, you can griddle your buns on the salt plate before cooking the meat.

¼ cup mayonnaise

2 tablespoons sweet pickle relish

1 tablespoon tomato ketchup

4 hamburger buns, split

1 tablespoon unsalted butter, melted

1 lb ground beef

Freshly ground black pepper

4 slices cheddar cheese

Sliced tomatoes, sliced red onion, and iceberg lettuce, for serving

1 Place the salt plate on the cooking grate over 1 burner of a 2-burner gas grill and turn on the burner to low heat. (If using a charcoal grill, see page 11 for instructions.) Cover the grill and warm until the internal temperature of the grill reaches 250°F, about 15 minutes. Increase the heat to medium and warm until the internal temperature of the grill reaches 400°F, 15–20 minutes longer. Turn on the second burner to low.

2 In a bowl, stir together the mayonnaise, pickle relish, and ketchup to make a sauce. Brush the cut halves of the buns with melted butter. Divide the beef into 4 equal portions and form each into a patty about 5 inches in diameter and ⅛ inch thick. Season the patties with pepper.

3 Place the buns, cut sides down, directly on the grill over low heat until lightly toasted, about 1 minute; set aside. Place the patties on the hot salt plate, close the grill, and cook for 2 minutes. Flip the patties, place a slice of cheese on top of each, close the grill, and continue to cook until the cheese is melted and the bottom of the patties are well seared, about 2 minutes longer.

4 Spread the sauce on both sides of each bun. Place a cheese-topped patty on the bottom of each bun, top with sliced tomatoes, red onion, and lettuce, and cover with the bun top. Serve right away.

SERVES 4

Steak au Poivre with Salt-Cooked Mushrooms

Cooking the steak on the salt plate provides an evenly browned crust without being overly salty, providing a balanced pairing with the well seasoned mushrooms. For a well-rounded meal, serve with Smashed Potatoes with Chimichurri (page 19) and a tossed green salad.

1 Set the salt plate on top of a gas burner on the stove top and turn on the heat to low. Warm the plate for 15 minutes. Increase the heat to medium and warm for 15 minutes. Increase the heat to medium-high and warm for 15 more minutes, for a total of 45 minutes.

2 Place the peppercorns in a large re-sealable plastic bag, press out the air, and seal the bag. Place the bag on a cutting board and use a sturdy frying pan to crush the peppercorns coarsely. Using your fingertips, press the peppercorns into one side of each filet mignon, dividing evenly. In a bowl, combine the mushrooms, shallot, thyme, ground pepper, and oil until evenly coated.

3 Place the steaks peppercorn-side down on the hot salt plate and cook for 5 minutes. Flip the steaks peppercorn-side up and cook until well browned on the other side, about 5 minutes. Using tongs, turn the steaks on their sides and sear until well browned on all sides, about 2 minutes total. Transfer to a plate and let rest for about 10 minutes.

4 Place the mushrooms on the salt plate and cook, stirring occasionally, until the mushrooms have released their liquid and are lightly browned and tender, about 6 minutes. Serve alongside the steaks.

SERVES 2

2 teaspoons whole black peppercorns, plus ¼ teaspoon freshly ground pepper

2 filet mignons, each about 8 oz and 2 inches thick

8 oz assorted mushrooms, cut, if necessary, into ¼-inch slices

2 tablespoons thinly sliced shallot

½ teaspoon chopped fresh thyme

1 tablespoon olive oil

Beef Teppanyaki, Salt Plate–Style

Teppanyaki is a style of Japanese cooking that involves grilling or stir-frying food on a flat metal griddle or iron plate. In this take on the recipe, thinly sliced steak, marinated with sesame oil, garlic, ginger, and other seasonings, is quickly seared on a salt plate.

1½ tablespoons toasted sesame oil

1½ tablespoons canola oil, plus more for brushing

1½ teaspoons minced garlic

¼ cup thinly sliced green onions

2 teaspoons freshly grated ginger

2 tablespoons sugar

2 New York strip steaks, each about 10 oz and 1 inch thick, thinly sliced

½ red onion, thinly sliced

1 large jalapeño chile, thinly sliced into rounds

1 Place the salt plate on the cooking grate of a gas grill and turn on the grill to low heat. (If using a charcoal grill, see page 11 for instructions.) Cover the grill and warm until the internal temperature of the grill reaches 250°F, about 15 minutes. Increase the heat to medium and warm until the internal temperature of the grill reaches 450°–500°F, 20–25 minutes longer.

2 Meanwhile, in a large bowl, whisk together the sesame oil, 1½ tablespoons canola oil, the garlic, green onions, ginger, and sugar. Add the steak strips, red onion, and jalapeño and toss until well combined. Let stand at room temperature for 30 minutes.

3 Lightly brush the hot salt plate with canola oil. Working in batches, place the steak mixture on the hot salt plate in a single layer and cook, turning once, until browned on both sides, 1–2 minutes per side. Transfer the cooked steak mixture to a warmed serving dish. Continue to cook the remaining steak mixture, brushing the salt plate with more canola oil between batches. Serve right away.

SERVES 4

Salted Chocolate Chip Cookies

These cookies bake on a preheated salt plate, which imparts a subtle saltiness while creating very crisp bottoms. We like a mixture of equal parts bittersweet, semisweet, and milk chocolate chips, but any combination or single type of chocolate chips will work nicely.

1 Place the salt plate on an oven rack set in the bottom third of the oven. Preheat the oven to 375°F and set a timer for 1 hour and 15 minutes.

2 About 15 minutes before the salt plate is ready, in a bowl, whisk together the flour, salt, and baking soda. In a stand mixer fitted with the paddle attachment, beat the butter, brown sugar, and granulated sugar on medium speed until light and fluffy, 3–4 minutes, stopping occasionally to scrape down the bowl. Add the vanilla, whole egg, and egg yolk and beat until incorporated, about 1 minute. Reduce the speed to low, add the flour mixture, and beat just until smooth, about 1 minute, stopping occasionally to scrape down the bowl. Using a rubber spatula, stir in the chocolate chips.

3 Shape the dough into 24 equal balls, about 2 tablespoons each. Carefully remove the hot salt plate from the oven and place on a wire rack set on the counter. Place 6 dough balls, evenly spaced, on the salt plate and lightly press each down with the back of a metal spatula. Return the salt plate to the oven and bake until the cookie edges are browned and centers are just set, 8–9 minutes. Transfer the salt plate to a rack and let the cookies stand for 2 minutes. Transfer the cookies to another cooling rack. Immediately start the next batch of cookies, placing 6 more dough balls on the plate, and repeating the baking process with the remaining dough.

MAKES 24 COOKIES

2¼ cups all-purpose flour

¾ teaspoon table salt

¾ teaspoon baking soda

14 tablespoons (1¾ sticks) unsalted butter, cut into ½-inch pieces

1½ cups firmly packed dark brown sugar

¼ cup granulated sugar

2 teaspoons vanilla extract

1 whole egg plus 1 egg yolk

12 oz chocolate chips or chunks (see Note)

TIP

For best results, have all of your ingredients at room temperature before you start.

Salt Roof Sundae

This play on a tin roof sundae can also be used as a template for your own frozen concoctions: simply swap in your favorite mix-ins for the peanuts and pretzels. Be sure that your ice cream is as cold and firm as possible.

½ cup vanilla ice cream

1 tablespoon prepared hot fudge sauce (not heated; do not use chocolate syrup)

2 tablespoons chopped honey-roasted peanuts

2 tablespoons chopped unsalted pretzels

1 Put the salt plate in the freezer and freeze until very cold, at least 2 hours.

2 When ready to serve, remove the salt plate from the freezer and place it on a cool work surface. Scoop the ice cream onto the salt plate, then top with the hot fudge sauce, peanuts, and pretzels. Using a rubber spatula, quickly fold the ingredients into the ice cream until integrated. Scrape the ice cream into a bowl and serve right away.

SERVES 1

=== TIP ===
You can make additional servings as long as the ice cream is very cold.

Salty Caramel Apples

In this recipe, apples are seared on the salt plate, resulting in a salty-sweet dessert or snack that is delicious topped with your favorite caramel sauce. This method can be applied to most seasonal fruit, but is especially good with apples, pears, and firm but ripe stone fruit.

2 apples, peeled, quartered, and cored

Prepared caramel sauce

1 Place the salt plate on the cooking grate of a gas grill and turn on the grill to low heat. (If using a charcoal grill, see page 11 for instructions.) Cover the grill and warm until the internal temperature of the grill reaches 250°F, about 15 minutes. Increase the heat to medium and warm until the internal temperature of the grill reaches 400°F, 15–20 minutes longer.

2 Place the apple slices on the hot salt plate and cook for 1–2 minutes. Flip the apples and cook until the apples are browned and soft, 1–2 minutes more.

3 Transfer the apples to individual bowls and serve with a drizzle of caramel sauce.

SERVES 2

Salted Chocolate-Almond Bark

The addition of a little salt to chocolate helps bring out its natural flavor. In this recipe, the salt plate gives the bark a welcome hint of subtle saltiness. If a chunk of salt has broken off your salt plate, feel free to grate it over the bark for an extra dose of salty flavor.

1 Place the chocolate in a glass bowl set over (not touching) a saucepan of simmering water. Heat, stirring often, until the chocolate is melted and smooth. Stir in three-fourths of the almonds.

2 Pour the chocolate-almond mixture onto a salt plate. Use a rubber spatula to spread out the chocolate mixture into a ¼-inch-thick layer. Sprinkle the remaining ¼ cup almonds on top.

3 Let the chocolate mixture sit on the salt plate to cool and firm overnight. When ready to serve, gently chip off pieces of the chocolate bark from the salt plate and enjoy.

SERVES 6–8

12 oz semisweet or milk chocolate, roughly chopped

1 cup whole unsalted almonds, toasted and roughly chopped

Index

The Salt Plate Cookbook

Conceived and produced by Weldon Owen, Inc.
In collaboration with Williams-Sonoma, Inc.
3250 Van Ness Avenue, San Francisco, CA 94109

A WELDON OWEN PRODUCTION

1045 Sansome Street, Suite 100
San Francisco, CA 94111
www.weldonowen.com

Printed and bound by 1010 Printing Ltd, China

First printed in 2015
10 9 8 7 6 5 4 3 2 1

Library of Congress Cataloging-in-Publication
data is available.

ISBN 13: 978-1-61628-971-3
ISBN 10: 1-61628-971-6

WELDON OWEN, INC.

President & Publisher Roger Shaw
SVP, Sales & Marketing Amy Kaneko
Finance Manager Philip Paulick

Associate Publisher Jennifer Newens
Associate Editor Emma Rudolph

Creative Director Kelly Booth
Art Director Marisa Kwek
Sr Production Designer Rachel Lopez Metzger

Production Director Chris Hemesath
Associate Production Director Michelle Duggan

Director of Enterprise Systems Shawn Macey
Imaging Manager Don Hill

Photographer Maren Caruso
Food Stylist Kim Kissling

Weldon Owen is a division of **BONNIER**

ACKNOWLEDGMENTS

Weldon Owen wishes to thank the following people
for their generous support in producing this book:
Adrian Hallauer, Isabella Martinez-Funcke, and Natalie Nesbit